DEAR STRONG FRIEND
A Guide to Grace and Breathing Again

A.L. Ember

VICTORIOUS
—BY DESIGN—

Plymouth, FL

Published by Victorious By Design, Plymouth, Florida.

Scripture quotations taken from the Holy Bible, New International Version®, NIV®.
Copyright © 1973, 1978, 1984, 2011 by Biblica, Inc.™
Used by permission. All rights reserved worldwide.
You can find more at: www.Biblica.com

Scripture quotations taken from the Holy Bible, New English Translation, NET Bible®,
Copyright ©1996, 2019 by Biblical Studies Press, L.L.C.
Used by permission. All rights reserved worldwide
You can find more by visiting www.netbible.com.

For more information about this book, please contact:

Victorious By Design
P.O. Box 638
Plymouth, FL 32768

www.victoriousbydesign.com

Cover design by A.L. Ember and Kelechi Kamalu using Canva

Printed in the United States of America

DEDICATION

For every friend who carries the weight silently, who shows up for others even when it's hard. May you find courage to lay it down, remember your heart is stronger than you know, and lean on God, knowing you are enough.

ACKNOWLEDGMENTS

This book would not exist without the gentle nudges of God and the people He used to remind me that my words mattered even when I didn't feel strong enough to write them.

To my Father in Heaven, thank You for being the One who sees me, sustains me, and never stops calling me *even when I'm empty*. This book is Yours. Every word, every pause, every breath between the lines.

To the strong friends in my life, you know who you are. The ones who carry burdens with quiet courage and still find time to check on others. You inspired these pages, and I pray they become rest for your soul.

To my close friends and confidants, your encouragement, late-night voice notes, and gentle reminders to *breathe* carried me through more than just this manuscript. You've held me together in more ways than you know.

To my parents, thank you for cheering me on when I doubted, praying when I couldn't find the words, and reminding me who I am when I forget.

To every reader, thank you for trusting me with your heart. Thank you for turning the pages and letting your own mask fall along the way. I pray these words feel like a warm blanket for your tired places.

And finally, to the version of me who wrote through her own weariness, thank you for showing up. This is proof that empty doesn't mean done. This is what grace looks like.

CONTENTS

Part 4: Living Restored

INTRODUCTION

You are the one everyone leans on.
The one who shows up.
The one who finds the right words when no one else knows what to say.

You are the strong friend.

But what happens when the encourager needs encouraging?
When the fixer needs fixing?
When the one holding everybody up else can barely hold up themself?

This is your permission slip:
You are allowed to be tired.
You are allowed to break and be loved in the breaking.
You are allowed to need.

You are not God.
You are not invincible.

You are human.

And you are still deeply loved; not because you are strong, but because you are His.

This is your safe space to lay it down.

Welcome.

Part 1: The Weight We Carry
Acknowledging the hidden burdens

CHAPTER ONE

"When I'm Fine" Is A Lie

I have a PhD in pretending.

I've lost count of how many times I said, 'I'm fine' when I wasn't. Sometimes, I even said it so convincingly that I almost believed it myself. Because when you're the strong one, admitting you're not okay can feel like betraying everything people expect from you.

There were days I wanted to cry.

Days I kept showing up for everyone else, even while secretly wondering if anyone would show up for me.

Days when I needed someone to ask, "Are you really okay?" and stay long enough to hear the truth.

But when no one asked I just kept carrying it all.

Because that's what strong friends do, right?

We carry it.

We smile through it.

We survive it.

And we say, "I'm fine," even when it's the furthest thing from the truth.

The Mask We've Mastered

Strong friends wear "fine" like an armour.

We hide behind it because we're afraid:

- Afraid of being a burden

- Afraid of being seen as weak.

- Afraid that if we really tell people the truth, they might leave.

Somewhere along the way, many of us learned that being strong was safer than being real. That pretending was better than the risk of being pitied, or the uncomfortable silence after you say, "I'm actually not okay."

But the truth is, it just isolates us. Pretending does absolutely nothing to protect us.

And the worst part? Sometimes, we pretend so long that we even start lying to ourselves; convincing ourselves that our pain isn't "that bad," that our loneliness isn't "that deep" or that our breaking point isn't "that close."

Saying "I'm fine" when you're breaking doesn't just hurt in the moment; it builds a wall between your heart, and the healing God wants to give you. You can't heal from wounds you refuse to name.

We weren't made to carry invisible battles alone. Even Jesus, God's perfect Son cried out in the Garden of Gethsemane (Luke 22:44). He didn't hide His anguish or paste on a smile. He fell on His face before the Father and prayed, "Father, if you are willing, take this cup from me."

If Jesus could be honest about His agony, why do we think we have to hide ours?

What God Really Wants

God isn't impressed by how well you perform strength. He's not looking for your polished answers, your perfect composure or your forced smile.

He's after your heart. Even the messy, tired, bleeding, breaking parts. Psalm 34:18 says, "The Lord is close to the broken-hearted and saves those who are crushed in spirit." He doesn't run from your brokenness but rather towards it.

Your honesty is not a disappointment to God. It's an invitation for Him to meet you where you are.

When Paul begged God to take away his weakness, He answered, "My grace is sufficient for you, for my power is made perfect in weakness" (2 Corinthians 12:9 NET).

Not in strength.
Not in pretending.
In weakness.

I remember once in my Christian journey believing that it wasn't okay to tell God I was angry with Him. I thought I had to filter my emotions before bringing them to the One who made me. That I should always come with gratitude, joy or praise; not grief, frustration or raw honesty. Even in prayer, I felt I had to be "fine."

But pretending before God doesn't protect our faith; it quietly weakens it. The more I tried to be okay for Him, the less I felt seen by Him. It was as though I was offering God a curated version of myself, one He never asked for. And without realizing it, I was slowly building a wall between my pain and His presence.

When we suppress how we really feel, even with God, we deny ourselves the healing only He can give. He doesn't need our filtered emotions. He longs for our full hearts.

Practical Step

You weren't made to carry life alone.

God created us for community; for safe spaces where we can tell the truth without fear.

If you feel like you have no one to trust yet, start by being honest with God. He can handle it all: your anger, your fear, your exhaustion, your questions. There's nothing you could tell Him that would make Him love you any less.

Next, be honest with yourself. Take time to reflect on what's really going on inside your heart and mind. Ask yourself:

- What am I feeling beneath the surface?
- Where am I pretending I'm okay when I'm not?
- What am I afraid would happen if I fully admitted the truth to myself?

Facing your truth internally isn't always easy, but it creates the foundation for honesty with others. Once you've done this, you'll be better prepared to share safely with trusted people in your truth circle.

When you feel the gentle nudge from God to take the next step, ask Him to bring you your tribe. It doesn't have to be a large group like the twelve apostles; initially, two to three people who have proven they can handle your truth without judgment is enough. Safe people won't be scared away by your honesty; they will be drawn closer by it.

Closing Charge

Dear strong friend,

Telling the truth might feel terrifying at first. You might worry that everything will fall apart if you let yourself be real. But the truth is, sometimes things have to fall apart so they can be rebuilt stronger.

You are still loved when you're not fine. You are still enough when you're broken. You are still held when you're honest.

Telling the truth isn't a weakness. It's the first step to true healing. And maybe, just maybe...it's the bravest thing you'll ever do.

CHAPTER TWO

The Silent Battles No One Sees

She answered every message, met every deadline, smiled at every coworker; all while silently falling apart.

She was me.

Dealing with functional depression was one of the hardest emotional and mental battles I've ever faced. What made it even harder was the fact that I was doing it alone. I had mastered the art of showing up while breaking down.

Hidden Weights

It took somewhere between three to four months of being a functioning depressoid (yes, that word is made up) before I admitted that I needed help. That admission opened the door to my therapy journey.

The root of this silent struggle wasn't just exhaustion or overcommitment; it was grief. After losing my cousin—who was the closest in age and had always gone out of his way to stay connected—and then one of my best friends to COVID just two months later, I felt invisible weights strapped to my chest. My best friend had been my rock and confidant; we had shared dreams, secrets, and life plans, including a promise I made to give my future daughter her middle name in exchange for her agreeing to be godmother. Losing her felt like a part of me had gone missing.

I was grieving quietly—the kind of grief that doesn't make you cry every day but makes meetings feel endless, simple tasks overwhelming, and your own body feels distant. I was functioning, yes. But inside, I was quietly unravelling.

I still remember my first counselling session. I explained my life as usual; showing up to work, keeping everything together, when my counsellor asked if I knew I was depressed. I laughed, half-joking, "Are you sure? I mean, I go to work, I get things done…" She smiled and said, "This is what we call functional depression."

It's not an official DSM-5 diagnosis or a clinical label. It simply describes what it feels like to function outwardly while quietly crumbling inside, living a life that looks fine on the surface while struggling beneath it.

Before that session, I had heard well-meaning Christians say things like, "Maybe you just aren't close enough to God," or "If you prayed more, you wouldn't feel this way." Those words stung, not because they were untrue in every context, but because they ignored the real, hidden weight I was carrying. Functional depression isn't about faith, or the lack of it. It's about a mind and heart quietly overwhelmed, even while life seems to run smoothly.

But that first therapy session was God-ordained, and it brought me freedom.

It was freeing to be reminded by another Christian that I did not have to suffer in silence. That needing help didn't disqualify me from being a strong friend.

If anything, getting the support I needed allowed me to become a healthier, more whole version of myself; for me first and then for others.

What Does God Really Want?

God was never impressed by my ability to "hold it all together." He wasn't standing back applauding my resilience while I crumbled on the inside. He wanted me. The real, raw, undone version. The one who didn't have the words for the grief. The one who didn't have energy to pray long, fancy prayers. The one who just needed to be held.

Somewhere along the line, we learned that being strong means never falling apart; but the Bible tells a different story. Jesus wept (John 11:35). Elijah begged for death (1 Kings 19:4). David wrote entire psalms from caves of despair (Psalms 57 and 142).

And still, God called them faithful. Chosen. Loved.

He never asked us to fake strength. He asked us to abide. And abiding doesn't require a mask. It just requires honesty.

Practical Step

I didn't wake up one day and suddenly decided to get help. It started with someone I loved looking me in the eye and saying, "I'm saying this because I care; you need to get some help."

There was no judgement in his voice. Just honesty. And grace.

So, here's my gentle ask to you:

- When you look in the mirror, do you recognize who you see?
- Can you hold your own gaze for longer than a few seconds without feeling the urge to look away...or break down?

If not, that's your sign.

Not that you're broken.

Not that you've failed.

But that you've been holding too much for too long, and it's okay to ask for help:

- It might be a conversation with someone you trust.
- A voice note you send because texting feels too hard.
- A first therapy appointment.

- Or even just writing out how you really feel. Without editing yourself.

- Small steps still count. Especially when they lead toward healing.

Closing Charge

You don't have to keep faking fine to be loved, seen or worthy. Let today be the day you stop performing strength and start practicing honesty. Even if it's just with yourself. God's not afraid of your truth. He's already there, waiting to carry it with you.

CHAPTER THREE

The Cost of Being Reliable

They know you'll answer.
They know you'll step up.
They know you'll "figure it out."

But do they know you're tired?

There's a special kind of exhaustion that comes from always being "the one." The one who stays late. The one who holds space for everybody else's breakdowns. The one who shows up— consistently, lovingly and without making it a big deal. The one people lean on, pray with, vent to …and somehow you always have enough to pour.

You're not unloved. You're not unsupported. But still the weight of being reliable wears on you in ways few will ever understand. That's the thing about being reliable. People stop asking if you *want* to. They assume you *will*.

Normalizing the Performance

Being the reliable one means you've mastered the art of functioning. You've learned to smile when your schedule is packed, to say "I've got it" when your cup is empty, and to show up even when your body and soul whisper, *stay home.*

And it's not that you're faking.

It's just that "I'm fine" becomes a habit, not a reflection. You say it because there's not always time to unravel. You say it because you don't want anyone worrying. You say it because, in some ways, it feels easier than explaining what's really going on.

But over time, that small phrase starts to steal something. Not just your honesty, but your access to help …your freedom to pause …even your ability to hear when God is gently asking, *"But are you really fine?"*

Why We Pretend

Sometimes we pretend because it feels safer to keep the peace than to be seen as a disruption. For strong friends, reliability becomes a kind of identity. People know you as the one who comes through; so even when you think about saying no, it feels like a betrayal. Not just of their trust, but of who you believe you're supposed to be.

You pretend you're fine because being needed feels like purpose. You pretend, because you don't want to disappoint anyone. You pretend, because slowing down means things might fall apart; and you've always been the glue.

But pretending doesn't make the weight go away. It just teaches you how to carry it quietly, until eventually, it carries you.

What It Costs Us

When you're always the one people can count on, it's easy to forget that you're human too.

You get praised for your consistency, but no one sees the anxiety you carry trying to keep everyone from being disappointed. You're admired for your strength, but no one asks how long you've gone without resting properly. You're celebrated for your heart; but few realize it's often running on fumes.

Over time, the cost of being endlessly reliable adds up in hidden ways:

- You begin to associate love with usefulness.
- You struggle to receive care unless you've "earned" it.
- You overcommit, then quietly burn out while still smiling.

- You begin to resent the very people you love, not because they're ungrateful, but because you never gave them room to show up for you.

And if you're not careful, your value gets wrapped so tightly in doing that you forget how to be.

What God Really Wants

God isn't asking you to be the most dependable person in everyone's life. He's asking you to let Him be the most dependable in yours. He didn't create you just to carry burdens, manage emotions or fix what others can't handle. You are not the back-up saviour. You are a beloved child: worthy of rest, gentleness and grace.

Jesus didn't just serve others; He withdrew to quiet places to pray (Luke 5:16). He let people wait, as when He delayed going to Lazarus (John 11:5–6). He even walked away when the pressure was great, slipping through crowds or refusing to be made king (Luke 4:30; John 6:15). At every turn, His obedience to the Father mattered more than appearances (John 5:19).

And you? You don't have to earn your worth by being reliable. God already counted you worthy when you were still breaking under the pressure. What He really wants is for you to come as you are. Tired, unsure, messy; and let Him carry what you've been holding alone.

Practical Step:

Before you say yes to the next request, pause and ask yourself:

1. Am I agreeing out of love, or out of fear of disappointing someone?
2. Is this a "yes" I can give without resentment or depletion?
3. Is God asking me to do this; or am I asking myself to be everything to everyone again?

Then try this:

Make a "Yes & No" list this week.
- On one side, list the things you've recently said yes to.
- On the other, what you've wanted to say no to but didn't

Look for patterns. Pray over this list. Ask God to show you where He's calling you to serve and where He's calling you to rest. You might be surprised how many of your yeses were actually quiet cries for validation.

Closing Charge

You don't have to prove your worth by being available 24/7. Your "yes" is sacred and so is your wellbeing. Let your value be rooted in being God's, not just in being needed.

Say yes when it's true. Say no when it's honest. And trust that the world, and the people who truly love you won't fall apart just because you choose to rest.

You're allowed to pause. You're allowed to protect your peace. And you're allowed to be held, not just helpful.

CHAPTER FOUR

The Weight of Doing it Alone

Strong friends carry an invisible weight: the belief that we must handle everything ourselves. It's not that we don't want help, it's that we often **don't know how to let others in**. We've never had another strong friend to model it. We've been the anchors, the problem-solvers, the safe spaces for everyone else. When our own struggles arise, we brush them off, thinking we can manage alone.

But some burdens; like depression, grief, or deep exhaustion, cannot be brushed off. They demand attention. They demand that we sit with them, face them, and sometimes let them be seen.

If you're a strong friend reading this, maybe you've held back because you're afraid of being perceived as weak. Maybe you've never had someone show you that it's safe to let others in. You are not alone in that fear.

The Moment That Shifted Things

I remember the day I finally admitted I needed help. I wasn't coping. I wasn't thriving. I was surviving on fumes. Starting therapy was one of the bravest things I've done for myself.

But what surprised me even more was what happened next. My goddaughter's father showed up, with chocolate. He didn't preach. He didn't try to fix anything. He just …showed up.

I may have told him and his wife I was in therapy. I honestly don't fully remember, but the point isn't the words I said. It's the fact that someone **noticed, cared, and simply arrived**.

Sometimes people do want to help. But strong friends are so practiced at hiding their needs that we don't give them the chance.

Why We Resist Being Checked On

Strong friends rarely ask for support, not because we think we're invincible, but because vulnerability feels unfamiliar, risky, and foreign.

We worry:

- If I fall apart, who will pick up the pieces?
- Will I be seen as weak?
- Will people still need me if I stop performing strength?

There's also guilt:

- Others have it worse.
- You're being dramatic.
- Be grateful; it's not that bad.

So, we shrink back. We throw ourselves into solving everyone else's problems, avoiding our own. But needing help doesn't make you a burden. Letting someone in doesn't make you weak. In fact, it makes you brave.

The Toll of Self-Reliance

Refusing to be checked on doesn't keep us strong. It slowly chips away at our soul.

We grow resentful. Bitter that no one sees how hard we're trying. Frustrated that no one sees how much we're carrying.

We burn out: emotionally, spiritually, sometimes physically. And the tragic part? People assume we're okay because we've trained them to.

We suffer in silence. Exhausted. Invisible. Overcommitted. Under supported.

And if we're not careful, we start believing the lie: **"If I stop being strong, they'll stop needing me."**

But friends, being needed is not the same as being loved. God never intended for you to live on empty.

What God Really Wants

God isn't impressed by your ability to hold it all together. He's after your heart, your honesty, and your surrender.

He calls us into **community**, to share burdens and receive care:

- The friends who lowered the paralyzed man through the roof (Mark 2:1–12)

- Esther asking all the Jews to fast with her (Esther 4)

- Even Jesus letting his disciples sit with Him in Gethsemane (Luke 22)

You are not meant to carry the weight alone. God invites you to abide in Him, to rest, to receive, and to allow others to help carry the load.

Practical Step

Take five minutes this week to do the following:
1. Reflect: "What am I carrying that no one sees?"
2. Write it down. Bring it before God without editing or sugarcoating.
3. Ask yourself: "Who do I trust enough to let in, even a little?"

You don't have to tell everyone. But maybe you can tell someone. Let one trusted person sit with you in your heaviness.

Closing Charge

You were never created to be everyone's anchor while you drown. Being the strong friend shouldn't cost you your soul.

You are allowed to rest. To speak up. To be seen. To say, "I'm not okay."

You are still deeply loved; not for what you hold, but for who you are.

Let someone check on you too.

CHAPTER FIVE

Strength Is Not the Same as Healing

I was doing everything "right", showing up, smiling, being dependable. But deep down, I was running on fumes. People kept calling me strong, but it didn't feel like strength. It felt like survival. Endurance is not the same as restoration.

We're often taught that strength means pushing through, carrying burdens, and powering forward no matter the cost. But what if that definition is incomplete? What if true strength lies in allowing ourselves to struggle, to surrender, and to receive the healing God offers?

Strength is not the same as healing; and pretending is not the same as peace.

The Cost of Mis-Defining Strength

When we equate strength with simply enduring, we pay a high price. Every time I relied on sheer perseverance instead of allowing God to heal, I chipped away at my peace, my joy and my capacity to receive grace. I confused surviving with being restored.

This misconception drains more than energy. It impacts our relationships, isolates us emotionally and leaves us numb rather than renewed. The more we rely on our own version of strength, the more we miss moments where God could have ministered to our hearts.

We also risk confusing our self-worth with performance. The longer we equate strength with pushing through pain, the less we recognize that true healing comes from surrender, not stamina.

The lie that "strength means I'm okay" is costly. It chips away at our wellbeing every time we push through instead of pausing. Every time we wear resilience like armour, it becomes harder to remove. We begin to associate our worth with how much we can carry, how quickly we bounce back, how flawlessly we can recover. But that's not healing. That's surviving.

And over time, survival mode starts to steal from us. It takes our peace. It drains our joy. It wears down our bodies, minds and spirits until even the smallest tasks feel weighty.

It also affects our relationships. The people closest to us may not know how to support us, because we've spent so long acting like we don't need help. We become more isolated in our strength, craving connection but unsure how to reach for it.

Eventually, if left unchecked, we confuse being "strong" with being numb. We stop feeling deeply; not because we're healed, but because we're tired.

Real strength isn't about pushing past pain. It's about knowing when it's time to rest, release and receive healing. And when we delay that healing, the cost isn't just emotional—it's spiritual. We lose moments where God could have ministered to us in our vulnerability.

Healing can't happen where hiding lives. Keeping up appearances doesn't always show outwardly; sometimes, it wears down our soul.

What God Really Wants

For so long, I believed that strength meant I had to carry everything myself. That showing up, smiling, and being dependable was proof of faithfulness. But God doesn't measure us by how much we can endure alone.

Take Moses, for example. He was responsible for leading an entire nation, and the weight nearly crushed him. But God didn't leave him to bear it all. Jethro, his father-in-law, advised him to delegate and to trust others to share the load. God provides support through others; He doesn't expect us to go it alone.

Romans 12:2 (NIV) reminds us, *"Do not conform to the pattern of this world, but be transformed by the renewing of your mind. Then you will be able to test and approve what God's will is—his good, pleasing and perfect will."* Strength and healing are not what the world tells us they are. Transformation comes when God renews our minds, teaching us that true strength often looks like surrender, honesty, and receiving help.

You don't have to perform invincibility for God, or for anyone else. He wants your whole self: the worn-out, tired, anxious and weary version too. Let Him carry the burden alongside you. Let others, who He places in your life, help shoulder the load. This is not weakness; it is wisdom and obedience.

When Moses accepted help, he didn't become less of a leader; he became more effective. In the same way, accepting help and allowing God to renew your understanding of strength and healing doesn't diminish your faith; it deepens it.

Practical Step

This week, give yourself permission to pause and reflect on your definition of strength:

1. Ask yourself: "Where am I trying to carry it all alone?"
2. Identify one area where you could accept help: spiritually, emotionally, or practically.
3. Take a small step: delegate a task, share a burden with a trusted friend, or simply tell God exactly how exhausted you feel.

Remember, like Moses, accepting help doesn't make you weak; it makes you aligned with God's plan for restoration and true strength.

Closing Charge

You were never meant to endure everything by yourself. Strength isn't the same as healing, and survival isn't the same as thriving. Let go of the weight you've been carrying alone.

Allow God to renew your mind and let Him show you what true strength looks like: surrender, honesty and receiving support. Take off the cape. Let yourself be seen. Let yourself be carried.

You are still chosen, even when you're not okay.

Part Two: Breaking the Performance Trap
Learning that strength isn't our identity

CHAPTER SIX

You Are More Than What You Give

It's easy to believe that being available, always saying "yes," and responding to every call or opportunity proves your faithfulness. But that's not what God asks of you. He asks for discernment. He asks for obedience, not overextension.

The Temptation to Always Be "On"

For the strong friend, saying yes can feel automatic. Your phone stays on past midnight because someone might need to talk. At church, you're teaching Sunday school, singing part-time on the worship team, ushering, and then someone asks you to join another ministry. The impulse is to accept everything and not let anyone down.

Every invitation seems urgent. Every request feels like it needs your immediate attention. And yet, God's assignments are not measured by how busy you are; they are measured by alignment with His calling. **Every opportunity is not an assignment from God.**

This truth may need to be heard again and again: saying no is not failure. Saying no is not laziness or lack of love. It is faithful obedience.

The Spiritual Muscle of Saying No

Discernment is a spiritual muscle that helps you distinguish between your obligations and God's calling. Saying no can feel uncomfortable or even disappointing, especially when others expect your constant availability. But it's necessary. It preserves your energy, protects your clarity, and allows God's guidance to move freely through your yes.

Consider Paul in **Acts 16:6–10**. At multiple points, the Spirit prevented him from going where human expectation or opportunity seemed urgent or impressive. He could have said yes to every request, every open door, every human expectation. But he trusted God's guidance instead. Saying no positioned him for the work that mattered most.

This teaches a powerful principle: obedience isn't measured by how much you do, but by **how aligned your actions are with God's purpose**. Saying yes to everything can dilute your effectiveness. Saying no to what isn't yours allows God to do more through your yes.

Why Boundaries Are Sacred

Boundaries are not walls to shut people out; they are spaces to protect what matters. Without them, busyness can mask God's voice. You may feel productive, but your soul grows weary, and your discernment dulls. Every "no" is an act of spiritual wisdom. Every choice to step back from overcommitment is an opportunity to invite God's guidance into your next step.

Practical Reflection

Take a moment to review your week. Where did you say yes out of obligation rather than alignment? Where did you feel stretched too thin? Ask God to show you one area where a "no" would open space for His work to flourish. Remember: **every opportunity is not an assignment from God.** Let that truth free you from the pressure to overcommit.

Closing Charge

You were never meant to carry every burden, solve every problem, or say yes to every need. God may call you to intercede for a friend in a moment, and that's beautiful obedience, but there's a difference between being available to the Spirit and being available to everyone all the time. Let go of the weight He didn't give you. Walk in the lane He's marked out just for you. Trust that every yes, given with discernment, carries more power than every exhausted yes given out of compulsion.

CHAPTER SEVEN

Permission to Feel Everything

The Breaking Point You Didn't See Coming

I didn't cry at the funeral.

I didn't cry when I heard the news.

I didn't even cry when the doctor flagged something that should've shaken me.

Grief had layered itself quietly, one heartbreak at a time. And because life didn't press pause, neither did I. I showed up. I worked. I answered calls. I smiled through everything. I said, "I'm fine," and I meant it—sort of.

It wasn't until a routine work call, nothing heavy, just a minor correction from my manager, that the dam finally broke. I hung up and the tears came fast, like they had been sprinting to the surface for weeks, begging for permission to exist.

It wasn't about the call. It was everything else. That was the moment I realized I hadn't just been holding it together. I had been holding everything.

I didn't realize how much I'd buried until something small unearthed it all.

Grief. Fear. Exhaustion. Even anger, all wrapped in silence because I didn't think I had the space to feel them.

Maybe you know that silence too. Maybe you've been carrying so much, for so long, you've forgotten what it feels like to just *feel*.

What It Costs Us

Emotions don't disappear just because we refuse to acknowledge them. They find other ways to speak: through fatigue, bitterness, numbness, or unexpected outbursts. Suppressing sadness doesn't make us strong; it just makes us silent sufferers.

We weren't created to carry everything alone nor to fake peace when we're falling apart inside. The more we stuff down our grief, anger, fear, and disappointment, the more those unspoken emotions erode our joy and distort our self-perception. We begin to think we're "too much" or "not enough," all because we never gave ourselves room to feel and process.

When we don't give ourselves permission to feel, we lose connection with our own hearts. And eventually even with God.

What God Really Wants

God is not intimidated by our emotions. He doesn't flinch at our grief or grow weary of our questions. He is a Father who wants our whole heart, not just the polished parts we think are safe to show Him.

David, the man after God's own heart, poured out his soul in the Psalms with stunning honesty. One moment he lifted his voice in celebration, rejoicing in God's steadfast love (Psalm 30:4); the next, he cried out in raw despair, *"How long, Lord? Will you forget me forever?"* (Psalm 13:1, NIV). He did not hide his sins, confessing them with trembling honesty (Psalm 51:1–4), and he brought his fears, failures, and frustrations unfiltered into God's presence (Psalm 22:1–2). In every lament, every plea, every burst of gratitude, he offered his whole heart, and God called it worship (Psalm 34:17–18).

Elijah, fresh from his victory calling down fire from heaven (1 Kings 18:36–38), suddenly spiralled into fear and hopelessness. Threatened by Jezebel, he fled and even told God he wanted to die (1 Kings 19:4). But God didn't rebuke him or demand more faith. He met

Elijah in his exhaustion, sending an angel with food and water to sustain him (1 Kings 19:5–8). Later, God's voice came; not in the wind, earthquake, or fire, but in a gentle whisper (1 Kings 19:9–12). God didn't rush him back into action; He met him in the silence, guiding him forward from a place of care and restoration.

That's what God really wants is not our performance, but our presence. Not our curated strength, but our unfiltered selves.

He invites us to bring our joy and our sorrow, our gratitude and our grief. To say, "Lord, I'm not okay," and know He won't turn away. There is healing in His presence; but only when we bring our whole selves to it.

Practical Step

- Identify one emotion you've been suppressing—anger, grief, disappointment, or even joy that you fear might be misunderstood.
- Write a short prayer or journal entry expressing that feeling honestly to God. No filters, no performance—just truth.
- Sit with God in that moment. Not to fix the emotion or make it disappear, but to practice being fully seen and fully loved.

Closing Charge

You don't have to earn the right to be human. Your tears, your joy, your confusion, your anger, they are not a liability in God's presence. They are an invitation. An invitation to come closer. To lay down the polished version of you, and to discover that the God who formed your heart, can handle everything it holds. You have permission to feel. You always have.

CHAPTER EIGHT

The Freedom to Fall Apart

There's a difference between feeling everything and falling apart. One happens when you name what's going on inside; the other happens when your emotions swell so high they crash through the walls you've built.

For a long time, I believed that collapse was failure. Strong friends don't shatter. Strong friends don't cry out in despair. Strong friends keep it together no matter what. But the truth is: God doesn't flinch when we fall apart. Falling apart isn't weakness; it can be an act of honesty, courage, and faith.

When the Heart Breaks

Jeremiah, the weeping prophet, poured his heart out to God with astonishing transparency. He didn't hold back his anger, grief, or fear. He wrote in Lamentations, "My eyes fail from weeping, I am in torment within; my heart is poured out on the ground because my people are destroyed" (Lamentations. 2:11, NIV). He didn't sugarcoat his despair; he brought it fully into God's presence. And God heard him.

Even Solomon, the wisest man who ever lived, spoke openly of life's emptiness. In Ecclesiastes, he confesses the frustration, monotony, and futility he observed, "I observed all that is done under the sun, and behold, all is vanity and a striving after wind" (Ecclesiastes. 1:14, NIV). His honesty didn't diminish his faith or wisdom; it reflected his ability to wrestle with life's reality.

Falling apart isn't a failure; it's a recognition that life can be overwhelming, that emotions can't always be neatly contained, and that sometimes we need space to crumble before we can rise again.

The Strength in Breaking

We often believe strength is holding everything together, carrying every burden, and never showing our cracks. But strength is not the absence of collapse; strength is the courage to fall apart and allow God to meet us there.

When we fall apart, we open ourselves to God's grace, mercy, and presence. We no longer hide behind composure or a carefully curated image of ourselves. We let Him see our fears, our doubts, and our exhaustion. And in that honesty, we find healing.

Reflection

What if falling apart doesn't disqualify you from faith or friendship? What if the true measure of strength is the willingness to surrender the façade and let God carry the weight you cannot?

What It Costs Us

When we refuse to fall apart, we risk isolation, exhaustion, and disconnection from God and others. We might be admired for our resilience, but we are rarely known. We might be respected for our competence, but we feel alone. Hiding our struggles may preserve appearances, but it robs us of connection, intimacy, and the freedom God wants us to experience.

What God Really Wants

God doesn't need our perfection or composure. He desires our honesty. Like Jeremiah and Solomon, He wants us to bring Him our full hearts: the despair, the confusion, the emptiness, the questions. He meets us in the collapse, not only in our triumphs.

Even in breaking, there is worship. Even in despair, there is presence. Even in exhaustion, there is grace. God's arms are not closed to the shattered; they are where the shattered find refuge.

Closing Charge

You were never meant to be the hero in every scene. You were never called to carry everyone and everything at the cost of your own soul. Falling apart doesn't make you faithless—it makes you human.

Let the tears fall. Let the mask drop. Let yourself breathe. You're not failing; you're freeing yourself. You're allowing God to be God. You're letting His presence, mercy, and healing reach you exactly where you are.

CHAPTER NINE

Jesus Wept. And So Can You

Maybe you've finally let yourself feel it: the sadness, the frustration, the emotions you've tucked away for far too long. But now what? Now that the tears have fallen and the mask has slipped, what are you supposed to do with all of it? You've admitted you're not okay...but how do you bring that to God without feeling like you're being dramatic, weak, or unspiritual? Especially when you're usually the one holding everyone else together?

Even Jesus, the strongest friend to ever walk this earth, wept. Not silently. Not stoically. Not with shame. But with full presence and deep awareness. His tears weren't a breakdown; they were a bridge. He wept and then moved toward the Father, not away from Him. This chapter is for the strong one who's finally feeling everything and quietly wondering: *What do I do now?*

The Reality of Our Humanity

We often speak of Jesus as divine, miracle worker, Redeemer, Son of God, and rightly so. But sometimes, in elevating His divinity, we overlook something sacred: Jesus felt. He wept. He grieved. The shortest verse in the Bible, "Jesus wept" (John 11:35), is also one of the most powerful. In just two words, we see that tears are not a betrayal of strength; they are a reflection of love and presence.

Jesus knew He would raise Lazarus from the dead. He had the power and the plan. But still, He allowed Himself to feel the sorrow of the moment. He didn't cry because He was powerless; He cried because He was fully human.

As strong friends, we often fear what our tears might say about us. We're afraid of how others will perceive us, or worse, how we'll perceive ourselves if we stop holding it all together. But Jesus didn't cry because He lacked faith. He cried because He loved, and that's the kind of humanity God welcomes.

If the Saviour of the world could stop and cry without shame, then maybe we can too. Maybe your tears don't mean you're falling apart; maybe they mean you're finally being honest. Fully human. Fully present. Fully seen.

What It Costs Us

When we bury emotions to appear strong, we don't just build walls between us and others; we build walls inside ourselves. Emotions that go unprocessed don't disappear. They harden; they sour. They distort how we see ourselves, how we relate to others, and even how we hear God.

You might still serve faithfully. You might still encourage others. But somewhere inside, something is shutting down. Unfelt grief turns into apathy. Suppressed sadness becomes irritability. Unnamed disappointment starts to look like cynicism. And suddenly your soul feels… tired. Not the kind of tired a nap can fix. The kind that settles deep in your bones. That's the danger of spiritualizing strength and emotional detachment: we start thinking that numbness is maturity. That silence is self-control. That having no response means we're doing "well."

But Jesus, perfect, sinless, holy Jesus, wept. Not just once, but often. He wept for Himself in the midst of others' pain, as much as He wept for them. If the Son of God wasn't too holy to cry, why do we think we have to hold it together?

What we lose when we suppress is not just emotional release; we lose the honest, tender communion with a God who isn't afraid of our pain.

What God Really Wants

What if God never asked you to hold it all in? What if tears weren't a sign of weakness, but of surrender? Think about what Jesus showed us in John 11, not just His power to raise Lazarus, but His willingness to feel deeply before performing the miracle.

What does that say about what God actually desires from us? Not polished strength, just honest emotion. We tend to think that when we're moved by someone else's pain, we need to be strong for them. We feel the pressure to hold back our own emotions, to keep it together so that we can be a source of support. But what if strength, in God's eyes, looks less like holding it in and more like letting it out?

Jesus shows us that sacred strength can look like tears. When He arrived at the tomb of Lazarus and found Mary weeping, instead of immediately jumping into miracle mode, He wept too (John 11:33-44). The God of the universe who knew He was about to raise His friend from the dead still chose to feel the grief in the room. He didn't just cry for them; He cried with them. That tells us everything about the heart of our Saviour. He is not a God who demands emotional suppression. He's a God who welcomes our heartbreak; even when it's ours alone.

You weren't meant to absorb everyone's pain and then pretend you're fine. You were meant to bring that pain, your own and the burden you feel for others, to God. He wants you to give Him every heartbreak.

This is where freedom begins: not in fixing everyone, but in learning to weep in His presence and then leave the weight with Him.

Closing Charge

You don't have to apologize for your tears. They are not a sign of weakness; they are evidence that your heart is still tender, still moved, still human. Even Jesus, in all His power and divinity, allowed Himself to feel deeply. So, you have permission to do the same. When the weight of the world; or someone else's world, presses on your shoulders, don't just carry it. Cry about it. Talk to God about it. Lay it at His feet again and again.

Being the strong friend doesn't mean being the dry-eyed one. It means being the honest one. The surrendered one. The one who knows where to go with all the pain: yours and theirs. So, weep when you need to. And then let God hold what you were never meant to carry alone.

CHAPTER TEN

Rest Is Not a Weakness

Before we dive in, let's be clear about what Sabbath really is. God designed it as a rhythm of rest for humanity, not as a rule meant to weigh us down. After creating the world, He rested "and was refreshed" (Exodus 31:17), not because He needed it, but as a model for us; especially for those who give the most, lead the most and carry the most. There is also a promise for His people: "There remains, then, a Sabbath-rest for the people of God; for anyone who enters God's rest also rests from their works, just as God did from His" (Hebrews 4:9–10, NET). Rest isn't optional and it isn't a reward for finishing your to-do list; it's a divine invitation to pause, realign and be renewed. For the strong friend, this truth can be revolutionary: even those who are dependable and always giving are called to stop and allow God to restore them.

Understanding Sabbath isn't just about rules; it's about living that pause in the real world. Even those we look up to for guidance need it too. Even my therapist has a therapist.

One of the most insightful things my therapist ever told me was this: *"I have a therapist too."* At first, I was surprised. Weren't therapists supposed to have it all together? But in that moment, something clicked: strength isn't the absence of need, it's the courage to tend to your soul. Her confession didn't diminish my trust in her. If anything, it deepened it. It reminded me that even the people we run to for help need safe spaces to lay their own burdens down.

Some of us are used to being the helper, the counsellor, the strong one, that we've internalized the lie that we don't get to rest. But even the best physicians need healing. Even the strongest friends need sabbath. Rest isn't a reward for those who finish everything; it's a rhythm God designed for those who are still healing.

Not Lazy, Just Obedient: Holy Rest, Human Need

In a world that praises the strong, the resilient and those who push through no matter what, rest often feels like a luxury, especially for the strong friend. The one who everyone relies on, the one who always has it together. We've been conditioned to believe that rest is a sign of laziness, that it's only for those who have nothing left to give. But God didn't rest because He was tired. After creating the world, He rested on the seventh day (Genesis 2:2–3), not out of fatigue, but because He knew we would need it. He knew the strong, the dependable, the ones who always give themselves, would need rest too. And so, He gave us the perfect example.

God's rest wasn't about weakness or needing a break from exhaustion. It was a divine illustration, a holy pause to demonstrate balance and care for His creation; and we as His image bearers are called to do the same. The strong friend needs rest just as much as anyone else, but it's not always easy to take. We've spent so much time pouring into others that we forget we are human too. But just as God rested to set an example, He invites us to follow His lead, to rest, not because we're lazy or weak, but because rest is a command. "Remember the Sabbath day by keeping it holy. Six days you shall labour and do all your work, but the seventh day is a Sabbath to the Lord your God" (Exodus 20:8–10, NET). It's a command that acknowledges our human need for renewal.

Rest isn't a reward for what we've done. It's a command, a necessary practice that reminds us that we aren't defined by our productivity or our ability to hold things together. The strong friend needs to rest, not just for their own wellbeing, but because it's an act of obedience to God's design. We can't pour from an empty cup, and when we rest, we're reminded that God sustains us, not our own striving. Just as God showed us through His own rest, we can trust that stopping, pausing and refreshing ourselves is exactly what we need to keep going. It's not lazy; it's holy.

What It Costs Us: The Hidden Price of Ignoring Rest

When we refuse to rest, the cost isn't always immediate, but it is inevitable. The most obvious toll comes in the form of physical exhaustion; our bodies will only carry so much weight before they start to break down. You might feel it in the form of frequent colds, unexplained fatigue, headaches or muscle aches. It shows up when your body forces you to rest by getting sick or shutting down. But the physical signs are just the surface.

Emotionally, the price is even higher. Without rest, we start to feel drained, overwhelmed, and distant from the things and people we love; the very people we hold space for. It's the constant feeling of being on the edge of burnout, but never fully able to reset. Stress builds up until it manifests in irritability, impatience, or even a sense of numbness where we can't find the energy to care. And that's when the body begins to demand the rest we've neglected through more serious symptoms, whether it's an illness, exhaustion or even anxiety attacks that take us by surprise.

The emotional and physical toll of not resting is not just about being tired. It's about being disconnected from ourselves. It's that feeling of knowing you're doing everything you can but still not being able to fully show up for yourself or others. The consequences aren't always visible at first, they accumulate, quietly eroding our peace of mind, our health and our ability to be present in our relationships. It's a slow burn that leads to complete exhaustion, and we can only ignore it for so long before it demands our attention.

What God Really Wants

Rest. Naturally, that one word would sum up this entire section, but I'd be doing you a disservice and being disobedient if I didn't expound just a little. God's call to rest isn't a commandment that weighs us down with guilt or pressure and it's not meant to be twisted into another point of legalism. We see in Scripture that when the Pharisees tried to trap Jesus for healing on the Sabbath, He reminded them that "The Sabbath was made for man, not man for the Sabbath" (Mark 2:27, NET). Rest isn't just a rule; it's an invitation and a gift from God to help us recharge, realign and renew. We don't rest because we've earned it; we rest because God loves us enough to provide it.

Don't fall into the trap of thinking that rest is only for the "perfect" moments when you have nothing left to give. Rest is the opportunity God gives us to say, "I trust You," even in the busiest seasons. It's not about measuring how "good" we've been or fearing that we're not doing enough. Rest is part of the rhythm of grace: freely offered and deeply needed.

Embracing the Rest You Need

Rest isn't just about sleeping. It's about honouring your body, mind and spirit by taking time to recharge. It's not a luxury, it's a necessity.

Start Small:

- **Schedule your rest:** pick one day or even a few hours in the week where you can truly unplug. Set boundaries around your time; say "no" to things that drain you and say "yes" to quiet moments with God. It might be as simple as a no-tech Sunday or an evening where you spend time reflecting or journaling.

- **Listen to your body:** notice when you're feeling physically or emotionally drained. Often, we push through these signals, but true strength comes from acknowledging that rest is necessary for renewal. Give yourself permission to rest without guilt.

- **Create a restful environment:** whether it's a cozy corner for reading, dimming the lights to wind down at night, or playing soft worship music, create an atmosphere that invites peace and rest.

The Point: it's not about checking off a box but rather aligning your actions with God's example of rest. Remember, your purpose will be far more sustainable when you honour the rhythm of rest in your life.

Closing Charge

As we close this chapter, remember that rest is not just a command; it's an invitation to live with the grace and peace God has already given you. Your strength doesn't come from doing it all; your true strength comes from trusting in the rhythm of rest He has set for you. Embrace it.

You don't have to carry everything alone. You don't have to have to keep pushing yourself past your limits. God is inviting you to rest in His grace, to fall apart in His presence and to be restored by the only One who can renew you.

Now, take a step back, breathe deeply and allow His peace to fill you. Rest is not a weakness, but a beautiful display of His love and provision.

Part Three: Becoming Held, Not Just Holding Others
Learning to receive; not just pour out

CHAPTER ELEVEN

It's Okay to Need Help

Sometimes help shows up before you even realize you need it. A message, a meal, a quiet act of generosity; these moments catch you off guard. Your first instinct might be to deflect, to say, "You didn't have to," but receiving isn't indulgence. It's trusting that God is providing for you, often through people you may not expect.

I've noticed I'm much better at giving gifts than receiving them. When someone goes to great lengths for me, I sometimes shrink back, feeling awkward or undeserving. It's ironic, because my name loosely means "one who is to be pampered," yet I resist the very kindness that reflects that truth.

Even the strongest friends are sustained by others, by hands, hearts, and prayers that reflect God's care. Accepting help is not passive. It is faith in action, a recognition that you weren't created to carry it all alone.

God Provides Through Others

Scripture is full of examples of God's provision coming through people. When the widow of Zarephath faced famine, God provided through Elijah, ensuring she had enough flour and oil to sustain herself and her son (1 Kings 17:8–16). She didn't summon manna from the heavens or conjure food herself; she received what God sent through another human being. Her courage to accept provision saved her life.

Just like the widow trusted Elijah's instructions, we can trust the friends God sends into our lives. Their support might not look miraculous at first glance, but it carries the same divine provision.

Every act of generosity: small or large, is God reminding us we were never meant to bear burdens alone.

In the New Testament, the early church modelled this beautifully. Believers shared food, homes, and resources so that no one was left in want (Acts 2:44–45). Every small act of care became God's hands reaching into someone else's life.

Even in everyday moments, God often works through the ordinary people around you: a friend checking in, a neighbour offering a meal, a colleague sending an unexpected note of encouragement. These small gestures are God's provision for your heart, your time, and your energy.

A Moment of Receiving

Imagine this: a friend notices you're exhausted. Without you asking, they drop by with coffee and a listening ear. You feel a little defensive at first; after all, you're used to giving, not receiving. But as you sip the coffee and share a few worries, relief washes over you. You realize that accepting this help doesn't diminish your strength; it restores it.

This week, as you notice help coming your way, try this: when a message or favour arrives, pause and say quietly, "Thank you, God, for this provision." Even if it's a text or a cup of coffee, letting yourself fully receive it trains your heart to trust God's timing and generosity.

The Courage to Receive

Being helped doesn't diminish your strength. It reveals a deeper courage: the courage to let go of control, to admit that you can't do it all alone, and to allow someone else to participate in your journey. Psalm 68:19 (NIV) reminds us, "Praise be to the Lord, to God our Savior, who daily bears our burdens."

Sometimes "daily" means through a friend, a mentor, or even a stranger. Receiving, whether small or large, is obedience in action.

Practical Step

This week, notice one way help or provision comes your way. Accept it without guilt. Let someone hold part of the load. If no one comes immediately, remember that God often provides through the unseen: a call, a message, or a quiet nudge in the right direction.

Next, choose one act of generosity or support you've received recently and reflect:

- How did it impact your energy, mood or perspective?

- How might resisting help have changed the outcome?

- Can you fully receive without guilt or defensiveness?

Jot down your thoughts in a journal or share with a trusted friend. Receiving well is a practice, a way of training your heart to accept God's provision through others.

Reflection Questions

- Where in your life are you resisting help because you feel you should manage alone?

- What would it feel like to accept God's provision through someone else today?

- Who in your life has been an unexpected vessel of God's provision?

- How does resisting help affect your energy, your joy or your faith?

Closing Charge

You were never meant to walk alone. Accept the help offered to you. Receive the provision God sends through others. Let yourself be carried.

It is not a detour from strength; it is a truer expression of it. The courage to receive is part of living restored. Open your heart, trust the process and watch how God's provision through people strengthens not only you, but the friendships and communities you love.

CHAPTER TWELVE

Letting Yourself Be Carried

Strong friends are used to holding the weight. You notice needs before they're spoken. You show up, you carry, you pray and you solve. You are a safe place for others. And that's beautiful. But there's a hidden cost: when you refuse to let others hold even a piece of your load, you step away from the very design God intended for your life.

Resisting being carried often leaves the strongest friends quietly exhausted. Strength isn't about going it alone; it's about knowing when to let others step in, trusting that life was designed to be shared.

Designed for Connection

God never created us to be entirely self-sufficient. That was never the goal. From the beginning, we see a divine pattern: the Trinity in perfect communion (John 17:21–23), humanity created for relationship (Genesis 2:18), and even Jesus choosing twelve disciples to walk alongside Him (Mark 3:14). We were built for connection: not just vertical, with God Himself, but horizontal, with others.

Resisting being carried, whether by people or by God, is not strength. It is a form of disobedience. It is saying, in effect, "I can do this on my own," when God designed life to be shared, held, and supported. Surrender isn't always dramatic; often, it is a quiet, daily choice to admit, "I cannot carry all this alone," and then to step into the hands God has placed around you.

The Strength in Surrender

Letting yourself be carried is an act of courage. It requires humility to let someone else speak into your life, to accept counsel, to receive prayer and to allow others to shoulder part of the burden you've been holding so fiercely. Proverbs 11:14 reminds us, "Where there is no guidance, a people falls, but in an abundance of counsellors there is safety" (NIV).

Even the strongest friends need wisdom, perspective and support. Allowing others to participate in your journey opens the door to guidance, encouragement and relief, and it aligns with God's design for mutual care.

A Moment of Receiving Accountability

Think of someone gently pointing out a blind spot; perhaps something you've been overlooking about your health, emotions or daily habits. Your first reaction might be defensiveness but pausing to listen and receive their words as a gift can lighten your load. Their presence and perspective can help you see clearly and move forward with freedom.

Life is meant to be shared. Burdens are meant to be lifted together. When you allow others to participate in your journey, you are not just receiving help; you are joining in God's design for obedience, community and grace. 2 Corinthians 1:3–4 says,

"Blessed be the God and Father of our Lord Jesus Christ, the Father of mercies and God of all comfort, who comforts us in all our affliction, so that we may be able to comfort those who are in any affliction with the comfort with which we ourselves are comforted by God" (NIV).

Letting yourself be carried allows this cycle of comfort and care to continue.

Practical Step

This week, notice one area where you are resisting being carried. It could be a worry, a decision, a task or an emotional weight. Choose one trusted friend, mentor or spiritual guide to share it with, remembering to bring it fully to God. Let yourself release the need to hold it all alone.

Practice surrender, even in small moments. For instance, accept guidance on a decision, share a worry you usually carry alone or let someone help with a task. Notice how it feels to rest in God's provision and in the hands He has placed around you.

Reflection Questions

- Who in your life could you invite to help carry part of your load?

- How does it feel to release control and accept guidance or accountability?

- What would surrendering daily look like for you in practical terms?

- Where do you resist receiving because of pride, fear, or habit?

- How might allowing others to participate strengthen your faith and your relationships?

Closing Charge

You were never meant to walk alone. Letting yourself be carried is not weakness; it is obedience. It is trusting God enough to receive, humble enough to let others participate, and brave enough to admit you cannot do it all on your own.

Surrender is the true strength of a strong friend. Step into it today and watch how God uses the hands and hearts around you to lift both your burdens and your spirit.

CHAPTER THIRTEEN

Healing Is a Holy Act

Healing isn't just a journey; it's worship. It's one of the most sacred things you can do with your pain. For the strong friend who's learned to press through, who knows how to be functional when broken, healing can feel like a delay, a detour or even a luxury they can't afford. But heaven sees it differently.

Jesus didn't just come to secure our place in heaven. He came to give us life: full, abundant life; even here, in the messy middle of grief, betrayal, anxiety, exhaustion and the hidden burdens of always performing strength (see John 10:10). Every step toward healing is a step closer to Him. Every layer of trauma, whether from past rejection, relational wounds or unmet expectations is an altar where God meets us. You are not weak for needing to heal. You are sacred ground in process.

What Are You Healing From?

Healing isn't abstract; it has a source. For the strong friend, it often begins with the hidden toll of carrying more than you were meant to. You might be healing from relational betrayal or from disappointments that cut deeper than anyone saw. You might be unpacking grief from past loss or trauma that never fully got attention. Or perhaps you're healing from the subtle but constant exhaustion of performance or the expectation to always be strong, cheerful and dependable, even when your soul is tired.

It could be a single traumatic event that shifted the landscape of your life or a lifetime of layered burdens that no one noticed because you were the one everyone leaned on. Maybe it's both. The point isn't to catalogue pain, but to recognize it, name it, honour it and bring it before God. Healing is the act of acknowledging these wounds, giving them space and allowing God's presence to meet you there.

Holy Ground in the Hurt

We rarely associate pain with the presence of God, but Scripture shows us that He draws near in our hurt. Psalm 34:18 (ESV) reminds us, *"The Lord is near to the broken-hearted and saves the crushed in spirit."* 2 Corinthians 1:3–4 tells us that God comforts us in every affliction so that we can also comfort others with the same comfort we receive. Even Jesus, after His resurrection, bore the marks of suffering in His wounds (John 20:24–29), showing that He knows brokenness intimately.

There's something sacred about our pain, not because God delights in it, but because He enters it with us. This section is for the strong friend who's learned to tuck hurt into quiet corners, waiting for the "right time" to heal. What if right here, in the ache, the unanswered questions, and the ongoing process, is holy ground? What if the very place you've been avoiding is where God wants to meet you?

The tears you shed, the frustration you feel, the confusion you carry, all of it is sacred in God's eyes. Being in His presence does not require perfection; it only requires honesty.

Why Moving On Feels Like Betrayal

Grief anchors us to moments, people and pain that once defined our lives. Healing, while desirable in theory, can feel like betrayal in practice—as if letting go of suffering erases its significance or dishonours the version of yourself that survived through it. For the strong friend, pain can become part of identity, the quiet reason behind resilience, the tenderness behind wisdom.

Healing invites release: release of justification, rehearsing old stories, the badge of "what I've survived." Freedom can feel terrifying when pain is the only familiar companion. But you are not betraying your past when you heal. You are honouring it, allowing it to rest and stepping into the life God intended. Healing doesn't erase what happened; it refuses to let trauma and grief be the sole authors of your story.

Why We Pretend

Strong friends are masters of the mask—not out of dishonesty, but responsibility. They protect peace, stability and others' needs while quietly crumbling inside. Vulnerability feels risky; past experiences may have taught them that falling apart leaves you alone. Pretending seems safer, but it isolates you from intimacy and support you were created to receive.

Deep down, strong friends long not just to carry, but to be carried. Not just to be admired, but to be understood. Letting yourself be seen in your brokenness is obedience to God's design for community and grace.

What God Really Wants

God isn't after your survival; He's after restoration. Healing glorifies Him in ways silent endurance never can. He wants to touch the wounds you've been hiding, to meet you in the places you've been quietly managing and to restore the wholeness He intended.

From the beginning, healing has been central to His heart. Jesus healed the leper (Matthew 8:2–3), called the bleeding woman to wholeness (Mark 5:25–34), and countless other examples are found in the Gospels and everyday life. These acts reveal a God who refuses to ignore pain. Healing is not selfish; it's sacred.

Practical Step

This week, give yourself permission to slow down and notice where you are still hurting, even if it feels small or long overdue. Ask God: *"What do You want to heal here?"*

Then do something tangible to honour the process:

- Write a letter to your past self and read it aloud with kindness.

- Replace one "I'm fine" with honest language when someone asks how you're doing.

- Listen to a worship song that brings tears, not for sadness' sake, but to let God meet you there.

You don't have to fix everything today. You just need to be willing to start, trusting that God is already at work, even in unseen ways.

Closing Charge

You don't need to apologize for needing healing. You don't have to rush through it or minimize your pain for others' comfort. Healing is not weakness; it is worship. Every time you choose honesty over hiding, every time you let God touch the tender places instead of numbing them, you participate in something sacred.

Your broken parts are not beyond redemption. God isn't asking you to hold it all together; He's asking you to bring it to Him. Let healing be your act of obedience, your declaration of trust and your response to a God who still heals, restores and makes all things new.

CHAPTER FOURTEEN

The Ministry of Empty Hands

We're so used to showing up with something in our hands: advice, resources, solutions, answers. For the strong friend, it feels almost unnatural to enter a space empty-handed. We believe our value is in what we can give, how we can help, who we can carry. But what if some of the most powerful ministry happens not through our offering but through our presence?

There's a sacred kind of strength in sitting with someone in silence. In admitting, "I don't have the answers, but I won't leave you alone in this." This chapter is for the fixer. The one who wants to hold the world together for everyone else but is slowly falling apart in private. It's an invitation to lay down the burden of always needing to *do* and to rediscover the power of simply *being*.

Ministry Without the Fix

You know that feeling when you want to help someone so badly, but you realize *this time*, you don't have the solution? Maybe you've been the person everyone turns to, the one with the answers, the one who always has it together. But what happens when your strength is running low and you're faced with a situation where you just don't know how to fix it?

We've all been there—when the people you care about need something from you, but you don't have the emotional bandwidth to give. Yet, the pressure to perform or to *fix* the situation, is still there. The lie we often believe is that being in ministry means we always have to provide the solution. May I offer an alternative? Sometimes the best thing you can do isn't to fix the situation; it's to show up, just as you are and be present.

Ministry doesn't have to mean having all the answers. It's about being a safe space, showing compassion and letting others know that they're not alone in their struggles. It's not about having the right words to say or the right solutions to offer. It's about showing up with your vulnerability and being present in the midst of someone else's pain.

Are you ready to shift your mindset and embrace ministry without the need to fix everything?

The Power of Presence

Consider Mary and Martha (Luke 10:38–42). Martha was busy with tasks, making sure everything was in order. Mary did something radically countercultural for their time, she simply sat at Jesus' feet. She didn't fix, serve or organize. She just showed up. And Jesus affirmed her choice, saying, *"Mary has chosen what is better, and it will not be taken away from her" (NIV).*

This is the ministry of empty hands. It's not about inactivity; it's about surrender. About saying, "Lord, I won't fix it. I won't carry it. I won't solve it. I'll simply be here, present, and available for Your work to unfold."

What God Really Wants

The truth is, God isn't calling us to be the answer for everyone or to carry the weight of others' burdens all by ourselves. What He truly desires is that we step into our role as His hands and feet, not as saviours, but as instruments of His love and grace.

God's ministry is never about perfection. It's about surrender. It's about offering our brokenness and imperfections, knowing that He is the one who heals, restores and transforms. What God wants is for us to show up, not as the fixer, but as someone willing to walk with others through their mess, reflecting his compassion, even in our own moments of fragility.

He doesn't need you to have all the answers. He just needs you to be available. To listen, to be present, to give love and to let Him lead. Ministry is less about solving problems and more about meeting people where they are, showing them the love of Christ and walking beside them in their journey.

Practical Step

Take a moment to reflect on the places in your life where you feel the pressure to "fix" things or others. Maybe it's a relationship, a friend's struggle, or even your own internal battle. Now, ask yourself: What would it look like to release the weight of fixing and instead focus on simply being present?

This week, commit to one act of ministry where you focus solely on being present with someone, without the need to provide solutions or answers. Just listen, offer support and remind them that they're not alone. Embrace the role of walking alongside them, as a friend, not a saviour.

Trust that God is in control and that, often, your presence alone can be a healing act.

Closing Charge

Ministry without the need to fix everything doesn't diminish your worth or your calling; it frees you to operate from a place of grace, not exhaustion. It's an invitation to trust that God is at work, even when we can't see the outcome. You don't have to be the solution; just be the presence.

As you move forward, let go of the burden of perfection. Ministry is about connection, love and grace, not solving every problem. Embrace the strength that comes from letting God lead and allow your heart to be open to what He wants to do, just through you, but in you as well.

CHAPTER FIFTEEN

God Loves You, Not Your Hustle

Strong friends are used to moving, doing, achieving. Hustle comes naturally because it feels necessary, even noble. You've been taught to give, to serve, to solve. And while all of that can be good, it can also become a subtle trap: the belief that God's love, or anyone's, depends on your output.

But friend, here's the truth: God loves you as you are, not for what you do. He delights in your heart, your presence and your willingness to receive, even before you accomplish anything.

A Moment of Receiving

Strong friends often carry everything themselves: family, work, ministry, friendships and don't even notice how tight their shoulders are, how stretched thin their smiles can be or how little rest they allow themselves.

When someone finally shows up to simply sit with them, no advice, no judgment, no checklist of "what I should do"; the impact can be profound. Just being present, fully received, can shift something inside. There's no need to solve anything, accomplish anything or earn anything. Just allowing oneself to be held, even briefly, can reveal a deep truth: God's love works the same way. He doesn't demand constant striving. He invites presence, being known, and rest in the fact that His love is never conditional on output.

Zaccheaus: A Hustler Seen

Consider Zaccheaus (Luke 19:1–10). He was a hustler, climbing the ladder, doing everything he could to gain attention and status. Yet

Jesus didn't commend his busyness or hustle. He saw Zaccheaus, called him by name and wanted to spend time with him. One night with Jesus, not a thousand deeds, changed everything.

This is the kind of love God offers you. He isn't measuring your ministry, your achievements, or your relentless giving. He wants **you**, fully present, fully known, fully received.

Receiving Love Frees You

For strong friends, receiving love can feel unfamiliar, even uncomfortable. You're used to being the provider, the fixer, the one everyone leans on. But receiving God's love and allowing others to love you too, is not weakness. It's freedom. It's surrender. It's stepping into the truth that you were never meant to hustle for God's affection.

Practical Step

This week, practice receiving rather than doing:

- Sit quietly with God and simply receive His love without a to-do list or agenda.
- Reflect on moments when you've hustled for validation and release them into His hands.
- Let one trusted friend pour into you: a conversation, a check-in, or a small act of care, and accept it without guilt.

Notice how receiving love changes your perspective. You are not defined by your output; you are defined by God's presence with you.

Closing Charge

You were created to be loved, not evaluated. Your value does not rise and fall with your productivity or performance. Let the strong friend inside you rest in the truth that God delights in your heart, not your hustle. Allow yourself to receive this love fully, and watch how it transforms the way you carry, the way you give and the way you live.

Part Four: Living Restored
Leading from a Place of Grace, Not Exhaustion

CHAPTER SIXTEEN

Safe to Exhale, When Stillness Heals

You didn't realize how loud the world was until you tried to sit in silence. No to-do list, no problem to solve, no one to rescue—just you and your thoughts. And maybe, that's what scared you the most.

Stillness has a way of bringing things to the surface: grief you buried, hopes you hushed, questions you never asked out loud. But it also does something sacred: it gives God space to tend to what your busyness kept covered. Not with noise or pressure, but with presence.

The world tells you that movement is the antidote to weariness, that the answer is always in doing more. But what if *rest*, not just rest in the sense of taking a nap or binge-watching a show, but the soul-deep quiet that allows for reflection, healing and realignment, is actually what your heart has been starving for?

This chapter isn't about collapsing from exhaustion. It's about learning how to rest before you break. It's about the power of stillness—the stillness where God can speak not to your productivity, but to your personhood. The stillness that doesn't rush you or require your performance but invites you to simply be. The strong friend doesn't just need rest. They need *permission to exhale* and to believe healing can happen in the hush.

You might fear what will surface in the quiet. But if you allow yourself the grace of stillness, you'll discover that in this space, God is not absent. In fact, He is right there, ready to heal the broken parts you've been too busy to notice.

The Cost of Constant Noise

Noise doesn't always come with sound. Sometimes it looks like a packed calendar, endless obligations, a thousand open tabs in your brain. Sometimes it's the compulsion to scroll when you're sad, to fix when you're tired, to say "yes" when everything is begging for a pause. Noise is the armour we wear to avoid what silence might reveal.

But over time, all that noise takes a toll.

It dulls your discernment. You start making decisions based on urgency rather than wisdom. You confuse motion with meaning. You become reactive instead of reflective. And beneath it all, your soul grows tired, not just from doing, but from never *being*.

The noise keeps you from healing because healing requires stillness. It numbs you from pain, yes; but it also numbs you from joy, from clarity, from peace. And the longer you live disconnected from stillness, the harder it becomes to hear God's voice when you actually need it.

Jesus often withdrew to quiet places, not because He was overwhelmed, but because He *refused* to be (Luke 5:16). He showed us that solitude isn't weakness; it's where strength is renewed. He knew the danger of a soul constantly exposed to demand but never given space to decompress.

So, here's the question: what is all this noise costing you? Peace of mind? Emotional clarity? A deeper connection with God? Maybe even your own sense of self?

You weren't made to run on empty or live in a state of constant distraction. The strong friend needs silence too, not just as a break, but as a lifeline. The hush isn't a void; it's an invitation. And if you can brave the quiet, you might finally hear what your soul's been trying to say all along.

What God Really Wants

God doesn't just want your service; He still wants your stillness. Not because He needs silence to speak, but because *you* often need silence to hear.

When life is loud and your mind is constantly rehearsing what needs to be done, stillness feels like a risk. For the strong friend, silence can even feel wasteful, like you're doing nothing. But what if that "nothing" is the most powerful yes you could give God?

Think of the Saturday between the cross and the resurrection—a day wrapped in silence. No signs. No wonders. Heaven didn't thunder. Angels didn't appear. Just waiting. But that quiet wasn't empty; it was pregnant with resurrection. Silence is not the absence of God, but the space where He is doing His deepest, hidden work.

God wants you to step away from the noise not as punishment, but as an invitation. To pull away not to disconnect, but to finally *reconnect*, with Him, with yourself, with the rhythm of grace instead of hustle. He's not in a rush, and He's not impressed by how much you can carry without breaking.

What God really wants isn't another finished task. It's a heart that trusts Him enough to *be still and know*, even when nothing around you feels certain.

Practical Step

Start with just 10 minutes a day. No music. No podcasts. No screens. Just quiet. Let yourself be still—not to solve anything, not to pray *for* anything, but simply to *be*.

This might feel awkward at first. You may even feel the urge to make the silence productive. But give yourself permission to resist that urge. Let this be sacred where you aren't anyone's safe place, anyone's solution or anyone's source of strength.

You are not abandoning responsibility; you are realigning with rest.

If emotions rise, let them. If nothing happens, let that be okay too. This isn't about results; it's about release.

Strong friend, you don't have to keep pushing to prove you're okay. In this silence, let God hold what you've been holding and remind you that peace was never meant to be earned.

Closing Charge

It's time to trust that silence is not your enemy. It's your opportunity for the deepest kind of healing.

In stillness, you're not abandoning anyone. You're not letting them down. You're simply acknowledging that your soul needs rest too. God doesn't need you to be on all the time; He needs you to be available to Him in all the spaces, especially the quiet ones.

You were made for both action and rest, for speaking and listening. Don't be afraid to give yourself the space to just *be*, without guilt or pressure. As you embrace the quiet, trust that is in the stillness that God will strengthen you in ways that noise never could.

You are safe to exhale. Rest is not just permissible; it is necessary. And in that rest, God is doing more than you realize.

CHAPTER SEVENTEEN

Sustained by Grace

Somewhere along the way, we mistook grace for a back-up plan. Something to fall into when everything else fails. But grace was never meant to be our last resort. It was meant to be our source.

This chapter is for the one who knows how to get things done, the dependable one, the steady one. You've been resilient, resourceful, reliable, but also exhausted. Not because you're weak, but because you've been relying on grit when God has been offering grace.

You weren't meant to survive on your own strength. Grace isn't just what saves you; it's what sustains you. It's not a last resort for the weary; it's the steady hand of God that holds you together, day by day.

Think of it like sailing. Your hustle may move the boat, but grace is the wind—the quiet force that does what your paddling could never. Or maybe it's like breathing: you can hold your breath and try to power through on your own, but you'll eventually run out. Grace is the steady inhale, the gentle rhythm that reminds you life isn't meant to be survived; it's meant to be received.

You don't have to earn your way through this season. You don't have to prove anything. Grace isn't a performance; it's a promise. And it's already yours.

Grace for the Journey Ahead

This isn't about falling apart anymore. You've done that. You've broken down, you've let go, you've learned how to be held. Grace carried you through the unravelling; not with shame, but with tenderness. Now grace meets you in motion. Not to drive you harder, but to walk with you wisely.

This is the season where strength doesn't look like hustle; it looks like margin. Where leadership isn't loud; it's discerning. Where showing up doesn't mean showing off and obedience doesn't always mean overextending. You're no longer driven by the fear of disappointing everyone. You're anchored in the truth that you are fully known, deeply valued and intentionally placed.

Grace is no longer just a lifeline when you're drowning; it's the compass that guides your steps. The quiet conviction that you don't need to prove yourself to be useful to God. You don't need to run to be faithful. You don't need to be exhausted to be effective.

This is the sacred shift: you're still the strong one, but now you're strong in a different way. Not because you never grow weary, but because you've learned to rest before you collapse. Not because you always have the answers, but because you know where to play your questions. Not because you hold it all together, but because you've placed your trust in the One who does.

You're not carrying everything anymore. But you're not empty either. You're full: full of grace, full of permission, full of peace. You're not hustling to be sustained. You're being sustained already, day by day, moment by moment, by grace.

What God Really Wants

God never meant for grace to be a contingency plan. It was always the foundation; the way we were meant to live from the beginning. The Christian life was never about mustering strength but about receiving it. We weren't called to just survive by grit; we were called to walk in the ease of dependence, to live fuelled by what He provides, not what we push through.

Grace isn't a gentle afterthought to pick you up when you fall; it's the sustaining power that was always meant to carry you. It is by grace that you were saved and it's by grace that you are meant to live (Ephesians 2:8-9). God's design was never self-reliance in holy disguise. He gives strength for the moment, but He also gives permission to rest.

If you've spent your life being the one others count on, it can feel unnatural to slow down, maybe even wrong. But grace flips the script: it says that God is strong enough to hold you *and* everyone else. You are not the glue holding everything together. He is.

What God wants is for you to live from His strength, not constantly strain to prove yours. To stop bracing for collapse and start building a life rooted in abiding. That's not weakness. That's worship.

Practical Step

What To Do (takes 5-7 minutes each morning)

1. Sit and Surrender (1 minute)
Sit quietly, palms open on your lap. Take three slow breaths, whispering: "I release striving. I receive grace."

2. Name Today's Weight (2 minutes)
In a journal (or the notes app on your device), write two short lists:
- Pressures I feel responsible to carry today.
- Places I feel inadequate or empty.
  Keep it raw and brief; bullets, not paragraphs.

3. Invite the Sustainer (1 minute)
Pray aloud or write one sentence after each bullet: "Jesus, sustain me here." Picture handing Him the weight as you breathe out; picture Him placing lightness in your hands as you breathe in.

4. Anchor in a Promise (1 minute)
Read or recite from memory 2 Corinthians 12:9, *"My grace is sufficient for you, for My power is made perfect in weakness (NIV)."* Let the words linger; underline the phrase that stands out.

5. Choose One Grace-Action (up to 2 minutes)
Ask, "If grace is carrying me, what single, concrete choice will reflect that today?"

Examples:

- Scheduling a 10-minute walk between meetings.
- Sending a "quick check-in text instead of composing the perfect encouragement novel."
- Accepting help on a task instead of doing it alone.

Once you've chosen your grace-action, write it down next to a checkbox and commit to completing it before the day ends.

By externalizing burdens and immediately exchanging them for God's sustaining presence, you create a daily rhythm of dependency rather than self-reliance. The single grace-action turns an internal shift into embodied practice, reinforcing that you truly are *sustained by grace, not grit.*

Closing Charge

You were never meant to run on empty or perform your way through pain. The same God who called you does not expect you to carry the weight alone. His grace alone is not a one-time rescue, it's a daily, steady source.

So today and tomorrow and the day after that, when your strength feels too small and your pace feels too fast, pause. Breathe and remember you are not being held together by your own effort; you are being sustained by a God who never runs dry.

Let grace carry what grit was never meant to hold. Let yourself be kept.

CHAPTER EIGHTEEN

Friendship Restored

I remember the text clearly. Tamara was stepping back from her role, and the Lord handed me the baton to lead the Thursday prayer group. It was a moment that showed me how living restored doesn't mean avoiding responsibility; it means stepping into it without performing for approval.

I finally learned that living restored doesn't exempt me from showing up. It simply means showing up with honesty, boundaries and God's grace, instead of a polished mask. It means no longer trying to be the strong friend who bends over backward for everyone at the expense of their own soul.

Leading from a Place of Healing

For the restored strong friend, leadership and friendship are no longer about performance. They are about presence. You show up with your whole heart, not a curated version of it. You lead not to earn approval, but to honour God's calling and care for others in ways that are sustainable.

This new rhythm looks like:

- Pausing to discern before accepting every responsibility
- Saying yes to what truly aligns with God's calling
- Allowing space for others to contribute and grow
- Embracing quiet and stillness as a necessary part of leading

In doing this, you begin to experience **friendship restored**. Friendships are no longer one-sided demands but shared spaces of trust, encouragement and mutual support. You can invest deeply without losing yourself. You can give without depleting, and you can receive without guilt.

The Scriptural Heart of Restored Friendship

God's Word reminds us that we are not meant to do life alone. Ecclesiastes 4:9–10 (NIV), "Two are better than one…if either of them falls, one can help the other up." Leadership and friendship flourish in connection, not isolation.

Proverbs 27:17 (NIV) says, "As iron sharpens iron, so one person sharpens another." True restoration means leaning on others as much as you allow them to lean on you. It's a sacred exchange where both lives are strengthened, not depleted.

Jesus also modelled this kind of relational and spiritual balance. John 15:15 (NIV), "I have called you friends" reminds us that closeness with God, and by extension with others, is built on shared life, not perfection.

Practical Steps to Lead and Love Restored

1. **Set Gentle Boundaries** – Protect your energy and clarity. Boundaries are not rejection; they are stewardship.
2. **Create Space for Stillness** – Daily quiet time replenishes the soul so that your yes carries power and your presence carries peace.
3. **Invest in Mutuality** – Identify relationships where love flows both ways and nurture those while respectfully stepping back from draining ones.
4. **Reflect and Adjust** – After leading, teaching or showing up, pause. Journal or pray: "Did I give from a restored heart? Did I lead from grace or compulsion?" Adjust your rhythm accordingly.

Closing Charge

Friendship restored and leadership from a place of grace are intertwined. You no longer need to perform to prove your faithfulness. You no longer need to exhaust yourself to carry everyone else's burdens. You show up, yes, but from the place of restoration, clarity and God's strength.

Strong friend, step into your calling restored. Lead, love and show up without burning out. Let your presence be a gift, not a performance. Embrace friendships that honour mutual care. Walk in the freedom of a heart unchained from obligation and trust that your obedience and grace-filled leadership will carry life, not fatigue, to those around you.

Step off the stage, strong friend. Walk into circles where love moves in both directions. Show up fully, with grace. This is what it means to live restored: to participate without performing, to give without losing yourself and to receive without guilt.

CHAPTER NINETEEN

Joy Comes in the Morning; But So Does Peace

You wake before the alarm. The room is still dim, but a soft band of light edges its way through the curtains, drawing a thin gold line across the wall. Last night's tears haven't fully dried; the ache in your chest hasn't packed up and left. And yet, something is different. The air feels less heavy, as if the darkness has loosened its grip. You breathe in and notice the inhale doesn't snag the way it did at 2 a.m.

This isn't the joy of confetti and trumpets. It's subtler, almost shy, like a friend who sits beside you in silence, letting presence speak louder than words. You don't leap out of bed ready to conquer the day; you simply roll your shoulders back and realize you can move without wincing. Peace has slipped in while the night was still prowling and now it lingers like a whispered promise: You made it through. Keep breathing.

Maybe this is what the psalmist meant when he wrote, "Weeping may stay for the night, but joy comes with the morning" (Psalm 30:5, NIV). Not necessarily a fireworks display, but the quiet miracle of still being here: heart still beating, hope still flickering, God still near. Joy may be on the horizon, but peace is already in the room, holding space until the sun rises fully.

Morning's Quiet Gift

We quote Psalm 30:5 like a promise of instant celebration, "Joy comes in the morning!" and imagine sunrise bursting through the window with drum-line energy and a worship-set crescendo. But most mornings arrive more gently. They slip in on tiptoe, offering peace before they ever hand us joy.

Think of dawn itself: it's not a switch that flips; it's a slow turning of the sky. First a hint of grey, then lavender, then the faintest wash of gold. Only after that does the sun finally crest the horizon. In the same way, God often sends peace as the first colour of healing—a hush that steadies the heart, so joy has somewhere to land.

If we expect fireworks, we'll miss the miracle. We'll wake up still sore and assume the promise failed. In reality, the promise is unfolding in real time:

- **Peace steadies our breathing** before laughter loosens our tongue.
- **Gentle hope softens the edges** before full-throated praise fills the room.
- **Presence comes first**, then emotion catches up.

Morning's quiet gift teaches us a new math: peace + presence = the groundwork for joy. When we honour that progression, we free ourselves from the guilt of not feeling "all better yet." We welcome the slow dawn, confident that the sun will rise at its appointed time—and until it does, peace is enough.

The Volume Problem: When Noise Masquerades as Joy

We live in a culture that cranks the speakers on every emotion. Weddings stream highlight reels set to swelling choruses. Testimonials crescendo in stadiums. Even Sunday worship sometimes feels like spiritual surround-sound: lights, drums, riffs. The louder the better. No wonder we start to believe that if joy is real, it must be loud.

So, when our souls settle into a quiet hush, we get nervous. We question our faith because we aren't dancing on the pews. We scroll past friends' jubilee posts and wonder what's wrong with us. We chase the next conference, playlist or podcast hoping it will pump up our volume, and confuse adrenaline with anointing.

But Scripture keeps whispering a different story. Elijah didn't meet God in the windstorm, earthquake or fire; he found Him in a "gentle whisper." Jesus slept through a violent storm because peace trumped panic. The resurrection itself happened in the pre-dawn hush while the soldiers dozed. Heaven's most transformational moments often take place beneath the noise floor of our expectations.

Here's the irony: when we turn the dial up on manufactured cheer, we drown out the very peace we're desperate for. Real joy has depth, not just decibels. It grows roots in the stillness, then rises strong enough to outlast the soundtrack. And if we keep equating joy with volume, we'll miss the quiet, steady pulse of God's presence already beating within our chest.

The Hidden Price of Chasing High-Volume Joy

When we equate "real joy" with emotional fireworks, we sign up for a treadmill we can't sustain. Mountain moments are glorious, and thank God, they're not in short supply. Yet even a steady stream of highs can't fuel every ordinary Tuesday. They were never meant to be our sole diet. Here's what relentless chasing costs us:

1. **Chronic Guilt**- every quiet season starts to feel like failure. Instead of resting, we interrogate ourselves: *Why am I not happier yet?* Guilt stacks on top of grief and heaviness doubles.
2. **Spiritual Whiplash**- we ricochet from hype to crash, conference to crash, Sunday to crash, mistaking adrenaline spikes for lasting strength. Eventually the crash feels worse than the climb ever felt good.
3. **Performative Healing**- desperate to prove the promise "works," we post hallelujah captions over half-mended wounds. But performance delays real mending; bandages don't knit bone.
4. **Shallow Roots**- loud joy can be like flash flooding: it runs fast on the surface but never seeps deep. Peace is the slow rain that sinks into the soil, anchoring us when drought arrives. When we skip the slow rain, our roots stay thin.
5. **Missed Intimacy**- God's voice often comes in the hush, not the roar. If we only chase the roar, we forfeit the close-up conversation—the healing that happens when it's just us and Him in the quiet.

Naming the cost isn't meant to shame us; it's meant to free us. Once we see what we're paying, we can decide to spend our energy differently. Investing in the unhurried peace that holds us long after the spotlight fades.

Biblical Nugget

Joy is not the same as happiness. Happiness flickers with circumstances, rising and falling based on what's happening around us. But joy, true, Biblical joy, is rooted much deeper. It is born from contentment, and contentment is the quiet soil where peace takes root. This kind of joy doesn't need noise or constant highs to prove that it's alive. It flows from a heart that has learned, like Paul, to be at rest in plenty or in lack, in clarity or in uncertainty. Joy is steady because it is anchored, not in outcomes, but in the unchanging presence of God. Where this is contentment, there is peace. Not the fragile peace that comes from things going well, but the kind that passes understanding. The kind that holds you when nothing else can. So, when Scripture says, "joy comes in the morning," it's not promising a better mood, but a deeper reality: that peace has done its quiet work in the night and joy is its sunrise.

What God Really Wants: The Gift of Steady Peace

God isn't asking you to fake joy or wear a permanent smile as proof of your faith. What He truly desires is for you to know His peace; that deep, steady presence that doesn't depend on your circumstances or emotions.

Peace isn't the absence of trouble; it's the assurance that no matter what you face, you are held securely in God's hands. It's the calm in the storm, the whisper when the world shouts, the rest that refreshes your weary soul.

Jesus didn't promise a life free from pain or sorrow, but He promised Himself, His presence, His peace and His victory over the chaos around us. When we stop chasing an elusive, flashy joy and start resting in His peace, we open ourselves to a healing that lasts beyond the moment.

God wants you to stop measuring your faith by how loudly you rejoice and start recognizing the quiet miracles of peace that carry you through each day. This peace is the foundation that makes joy possible, a peace that sustains you even when the noise fades.

Let yourself lean into this gift. It's not a sign of weakness or doubt; it's the heart of what it means to walk with God.

Practical Step

Tomorrow morning, before the day gathers speed, sit at the edge of your bed with both feet on the floor and let the stillness greet you. Whisper one grounding sentence: *"God, I welcome Your peace to settle me before anything else speaks today."* As you breathe in, imagine His presence filling the hollow places; as you breathe out, picture the worries of the night leaving with the exhale.

Carry a simple breath-prayer into the hours ahead—something short enough to repeat while waiting for coffee to brew or a browser tab to load: "Your peace, not my pace." Each time tension tightens your shoulders, let the words ride your breath, loosening the grip of hurry.

When the day winds down, resist the urge to scroll until sleep. Instead, trace the past hours like a gentle rewind and ask, "Where did quiet peace surprise me today?" Maybe it was a sudden steadiness during an awkward meeting or a laugh that lightened a heavy moment. Name one instance aloud, thank God for it and let gratitude close the night.

This unhurried rhythm; morning welcome, midday breath, evening recall, doesn't take more than a few minutes. Yet, it trains your heart to spot peace the way dawn gradually teaches your eyes to see light. Over time, you'll notice the sunrise of joy feels nearer, because peace has already kept watch through the dark.

Closing Charge

You don't have to force the joy. You don't have to stir up noise or energy to prove you're okay. Real joy, the kind that lasts, rises from a life anchored in peace. Let peace be your permission slip to slow down, your compass when joy feels out of reach, your steady rhythm when emotions won't cooperate. It is not lesser than joy; it is what carries you to it.

So today, release the pressure to perform. Let go of the guilt for not feeling "loud enough." And instead, let God's quiet presence meet you right where you are. In the hush, you are still whole. In the stillness, you are still chosen. Let peace lead, and joy will follow in its own time.

CHAPTER TWENTY

You Are Still Chosen, Even When You're Empty

I stared at the blinking cursor on my screen, fingers hovering over the keys that just yesterday, poured out encouragement for everyone else. Tonight, every word felt like sand in my mouth. The prayers I'd whispered on loop for friends suddenly lodged in my own throat. The strong friend, the reliable voice, the steady encourager...empty.

Under the hum of the desk lamp, a single thought echoed louder than my exhaustion: *If I have nothing left to give, what good am I?*

But then, quiet yet undeniable, a thundering whisper rose beneath the shame. A voice that didn't scold or demand but carried that weight of heaven:

"Beloved, I never chose you because you were full. I chose you because you are mine."

I let the words settle, felt them seep into the cracks my hustle had left behind. The cursor still blinked, but the panic eased. Maybe being chosen had never been about my capacity; maybe it was always about His. And if that's true (which I've found it to be), then even here, in this paused, breathless moment. I am still held, still wanted, still called.

The Reality Behind Feeling Spent

If you've ever felt utterly drained; like the well inside you has run bone dry, you're far from alone. The Bible is full of stories about faithful people who hit the same place, who felt empty and worn out in their service to God and others.

There's Elijah, who fled into the wilderness, ready to give up under a broom tree, convinced he was the last one left and that his efforts were futile (1 Kings 19). Naomi called herself "Mara" meaning bitter, when life's blows left her heart hollow (Ruth 1:20). Even Jesus' disciples faced moments after the cross when hope seemed fragile and exhaustion weighed heavy (Luke 24).

These stories remind us that emptiness isn't a sign of failure or unworthiness. It's part of the journey. Sometimes, it's the space God uses to reshape us, to draw us closer, to remind us that our strength alone isn't what carries the mission; it's His.

You're in good company. The strong friend, the encourager, the one everyone leans on—they all encounter this place where the light flickers low. And that's okay. That's human. It's real. And it's where God's grace meets us most tenderly.

Why Emptiness Feels Like Disqualification

When you're running on empty, it's easy to believe the lies whispering in the quiet moments:

- That calling means constant overflow, that if you're not pouring out every ounce, you're failing.
- That exhaustion equals weakness or lack of faith.
- That resting is shirking responsibility or disappointing God and others.

Hustle culture doesn't help. It prizes productivity and "grind" as markers of worth. Even sometimes within church circles, there can be an unspoken pressure to always *do*; to show up, serve and stay strong no matter the cost.

But here's the truth: God's call isn't a sprint with a finish line in sight. It's a lifelong marathon fuelled by grace, not by grit alone.

You're not disqualified because you're empty. You're human.

And in that human space, God's power is made perfect. His strength fills the gaps your own can't reach. It's not about pushing harder; it's about surrendering deeper.

The lies want you to believe you must always be full. God wants you to know that being empty is part of the process; and that He's never stopped choosing you.

What It Costs Us

When we carry the weight of always being "on", always available, always helpful, always strong, we end up paying a quiet price.

We hide our need.

We silence our weariness.

We tell ourselves, *Just one more thing,* even as our insides fray at the seams.

The cost of performing through emptiness shows up in subtle ways: the delayed text replies that feel like failure, the sighs we swallow instead of saying we're tired, the prayer requests we post for others while ignoring the ache in our own chest. Over time, it breeds spiritual burnout and emotional numbness.

And worst of all, it convinces us to suffer in silence. To believe we have no right to ask for help because we're the ones who usually offer it.

But that's not strength. That's slow erosion.

Unaddressed emptiness doesn't make us holy; it makes us more distant. From others. From rest. From the God who never asked us to hold everything alone.

The cost of pretending to be endlessly capable is high. But the grace waiting for us when we stop pretending? Priceless.

What God Really Wants

God has never needed your performance. He's never measured your worth by your output. What He desires most isn't a nonstop outpouring; it's a heart that's willing to remain close, even when it feels like it has nothing left.

In 2 Corinthians 4:7, Paul reminds us that we carry this treasure; the very presence of God, in jars of clay. Fragile. Cracked. Ordinary. On purpose. Why? So the surpassing power is clearly from God, not from us. Our emptiness doesn't disqualify us; it makes space for His glory to shine brighter.

God doesn't require fullness to call you. He asks for willingness. And when you're dry and dusted and discouraged, His invitation isn't to dig deeper into your own reserves. It's to abide.

"Abide in me," Jesus says in John 15, "and I in you…apart from me you can do nothing" (NIV). That isn't a warning; it's a mercy. It's God's gentle reminder that you're not meant to do this alone.

Psalm 23 doesn't say you fill your own cup; it says *He* anoints your head with oil, *He* makes your cup overflow. When you're empty, God doesn't pull away. He draws near to fill, to restore, to remind you that you are still His; even here.

You were never chosen because you were impressive. You were chosen because you are His. And He doesn't take His choosing back.

Practical Step

Once a week, Sunday evening or whatever moment feels like a gentle pause, sit somewhere with a quiet journal and a cup of something warm (something cold for me). Breathe deeply and let the week replay in slow motion.

1. **Name the Empty Place.** Ask yourself, *"Where do I feel most depleted right now?"* It could be parenting patience, emotional bandwidth, spiritual spark—whatever feels hollow. Write it down in a single honest sentence.
2. **Receive a Promise.** Flip to Scripture or recall a verse that directly counters that emptiness. "My grace is sufficient for

you," "He restores my soul," "The Lord will fight for you; you need only be still." Copy the words beneath your sentence and underline the phrase that lands in your chest.

3. **Invite a Co-Carrier.** Look at the empty place again and ask, *"Who could shoulder a piece of this with me?"* A friend, mentor, small-group leader. Decide on one simple reach out: text, call, coffee and jot a time you'll do it. Mutual care is a part of being chosen.

4. **Rest.** Close the journal, breathe out slowly and say aloud: *"I am still chosen, even here."* Then do something deliberately unproductive for fifteen minutes; sit on the porch (verandah for my Caribbean people), stretch, listen to music that steadies you. Rest is the exhale that makes room for fresh filling.

Repeat this rhythm every week. It doesn't take long, but it trains your heart to meet emptiness with truth, community and rest. The streams of grace flowing into the spaces your own strength can't reach.

Closing Charge

You don't have to be overflowing to be effective. You don't have to be loud to be heard. You don't have to be full to be faithful.

God's choosing of you was never rooted in your performance; it was anchored in His love. And that love hasn't shifted, even if your energy has. Even when you're dry. Even when your hands are trembling from the weight. Even when your prayers are just whispers and sighs.

He doesn't need your hustle. He desires your heart.

So, exhale. Let the masks fall. Let the pressure melt in the light of this truth:

You are still chosen. Still seen. Still enough.

Not because you're holding it all together, but because He is still holding you.

And that… is more than enough.

SCRIPTURE REFERENCES

Chapter 1

- 2 Corinthians 12:9 (NET)

Chapter 2

- John 11:35
- 1 Kings 19:4
- Psalm 3, 13, etc. (brief mention)

Chapter 3

- Luke 5:16
- John 11:5–6
- Luke 4:30
- John 6:15
- John 5:19

Chapter 4

- Mark 2:1–12
- Esther 4
- Luke 22

Chapter 5

- Romans 12:2 (NIV)

Chapter 6

- Acts 16:6–10

Chapter 7

- Psalm 30:4
- Psalm 13:1 (NIV)
- Psalm 22:1–2
- Psalm 34:17–18
- 1 Kings 18:36–38
- 1 Kings 19:3
- 1 Kings 19:5–8
- 1 Kings 19:9–12

Chapter 8

- Lamentations 2:11 (NIV)
- Ecclesiastes 1:14 (NIV)

Chapter 9

- John 11:35

Chapter 10

- Exodus 31:17
- Hebrews 4:9–10 (NET)
- Genesis 2:2-3
- Exodus 20:8–10 (NET)
- Mark 2:27 (NET)

Chapter 11

- 1 Kings 17:8–16
- Acts 2:44–45
- Psalm 68:19 (NIV)

Chapter 12

- John 17:21–23

- Genesis 2:18
- Mark 3:14
- Proverbs 11:14 (NIV)
- 2 Corinthians 1:3–4 (NIV)

Chapter 13

- Matthew 8:2–3
- Mark 5:25–34

Chapter 14

- Luke 10:38–42
- Luke 10:42 (NIV)

Chapter 15

- Luke 19:1–10

Chapter 16

- Luke 5:16

Chapter 17

- Ephesians 2:8–9 (NIV)

Chapter 18

- Ecclesiastes 4:9–10 (NIV)
- Proverbs 27:17 (NIV)
- John 15:15 (NIV)

Chapter 19

- Psalm 30:5 (NIV)

Chapter 20

- 1 Kings 19

- Ruth 1:20
- Luke 24
- 2 Corinthians 4:7
- John 15:4–5
- Psalm 23

A FINAL WORD

If you made it to the end of the book, I want you to know something:
You didn't just read these pages; you *lived* them.
You've carried hidden battles. You've shown up exhausted.
You've poured out when no one noticed.
And still…here you are. Still becoming. Still chosen. Still held.
This wasn't just a book. It was a mirror.
And more than that; it was a reminder that you don't have to live
hidden, exhausted or alone.
If this journey cracked something open in you, let that be the
beginning of healing, not just understanding.
Go back to the chapters when you need them. Scribble in the
margins. Cry if you must. Rest often.
You don't have to be the strong one all the time. That's not your
identity; it never was.
You are loved by a God who sees you, holds you, sustains you.
Empty or full.
This is your permission to live differently.
To receive.
To rest.
To be.
And maybe… to whisper to someone else along the way:
"You don't have to hold it all either. Come rest here too."

READER'S PRAYER

Resting in the Hands That Hold You

Father, I come to You just as I am no masks, no performances, no borrowed strength. You see the parts of me that are weary, the places that feel empty, the hopes that still flicker. Thank You for loving me here.

Teach me to breathe in Your grace and breathe out my striving. Settle my heart with the peace that whispers I am chosen even when I feel small, even when I feel spent. Lift the burdens I was never meant to carry alone and place them into Your capable hands.

Show me how to receive as readily as I give, to rest as boldly as I serve, to be held even while I'm holding others.

May Your joy rise quietly within me like morning light, steady and sure, growing brighter with each step. And when my well runs dry, remind me that Your well never will.

I am Yours loved, seen, and sustained. Let that truth echo through every ordinary day that follows these pages.

In Jesus' name, amen.

A NOTE FROM THE AUTHOR

Dear Reader,

These pages are for the strong friends, the quiet encouragers, the ones who pour out words of comfort even when their own hearts feel heavy. They are for those who carry light for everyone else yet sometimes forget to sit in the glow themselves. If you've ever felt the weight of being the steady one, the listener, the safe place for others to land, these words are for you. May they feel like a deep breath after a long day, a moment to be reminded that you are seen and deeply loved, right where you are.

May this book walk alongside you like a soft hand in yours, a pause in the rush, a gentle whisper that you were never meant to carry it all alone. May it point you back to the One who holds every burden without strain and every tear without judgment. As you read, may you find permission to rest, to be held, and to be comforted in ways words can't always capture. You have been the encourager; now let these pages encourage you.

With warmth,
A.L. Ember

ABOUT THE AUTHOR

A.L. Ember is an author and encourager who walks alongside those who carry heavy burdens while faithfully giving to others. She writes to remind readers that true strength is not measured only by what we give, but also by our willingness to receive, rest, and trust in God's care.

Her hope is that every reader will find comfort, encouragement and gentle guidance within these pages. She seeks to shine light on the quiet battles and small victories that often go unnoticed, offering words that restore, reassure and remind readers that they are seen, held and chosen even in life's heaviest moments.

When she isn't writing, A. L. enjoys journaling, reflecting on God's presence in everyday life and cherishing quiet moments with friends and creation. Each word she shares carries a prayer: that readers will leave her pages feeling lighter, renewed and reminded that they were never meant to walk alone, and that true strength comes from both giving and receiving with an open heart.

CONNECT WITH THE AUTHOR

I would love to hear from you. Please connect with me:

Website: https://www.alemberauthor.com

Instagram: https://www.instagram.com/a.l.ember

Threads: https://www.threads.com/@a.l.ember

TikTok: https://www.tiktok.com/@a.l.ember

Facebook: https://www.facebook.com/alemberauthor

Email: al@alemberauthor.com

COMING SOON

Jump – A story of faith, obedience, and the moment when you choose to leap, trusting God even when the path ahead is unclear.

Midair – Step into the tension between surrender and arrival, learning to fly before you land. A lyrical journey of waiting, trusting, and leaning on God's guidance.

Landing – When the waiting ends and life begins again. Discover what it means to stay grounded in faith after the leap.

Island Light Series – Escape to the Caribbean with stories of love, mystery, and discovery on islands where hearts are tested and truths are uncovered. Each book invites you to explore courage, faith, and connection in sunlit, sea-swept landscapes.

Stay tuned for more journeys to encourage, challenge, and hold you as you continue walking faithfully with God.

www.ingramcontent.com/pod-product-compliance
Lightning Source LLC
LaVergne TN
LVHW041232080426
835508LV00011B/1178